CREATURE FROM THE BLACK LAGOON

BY IAN THORNE
ADAPTED FROM THE SCREENPLAY BY
ARTHUR ROSS AND HARRY ESSEX
FROM A STORY BY MAURICE ZIMM

EDITED BY
DR. HOWARD SCHROEDER
Professor in Reading and Language Arts
Dept. of Elementary Education
Mankato State University

Copyright© 1981 by MCA Publishing, a Division of MCA INC. All rights reserved.
Library of Congress Catalog Card Number: 81-12468
International Standard Book Numbers:
0-89686-187-2 Library Bound
0-89686-190-2 Paperback
Design - Doris Woods

Library of Congress Cataloging in Publication Data

Thorne, Ian. Adapted from the screenplay by Arthur Ross and Harry Essex. From a story by Maurice Zimm
    Creature from the Black Lagoon.
    (Monster series)
    SUMMARY: Recounts the plots of the 1954 film and its two sequels which followed the career of an unfriendly half-man, half-fish creature discovered in a Brazilian lake.
    1. Horror films--History and criticism--Juvenile literature. (1. Horror films. 2. Monsters--Fiction) I. Schroeder, Howard. II. Title. III. Series: Thorne, Ian. Monsters series.
PN1995.9.H6T48   791.43'72   81-12468
ISBN 0-89686-187-2 (lib. bdg.)   AACR2
ISBN 0-89686-190-2 (pbk.)

PHOTOGRAPHIC CREDITS

Universal Pictures: Cover, 6, 8-9, 10, 13, 14, 17, 19, 20, 22, 23, 24, 25, 27, 28-29, 30, 31, 32-33, 41, 42
Forrest J. Ackerman: 2, 18, 34, 35, 36, 37, 38, 39, 40, 43, 44, 45, 46, 47

Published by arrangement with MCA PUBLISHING,
a Division of MCA Inc.

MCA PUBLISHING, a Division of MCA Inc.
100 Universal City Plaza
Universal City, California 91608

Published by
CRESTWOOD HOUSE, INC.
Highway 66 South
P.O. Box 3427
Mankato, Minnesota 56002-3427
Printed in the United States of America

14625

CREATURE FROM THE BLACK LAGOON

BY IAN THORNE
ADAPTED FROM THE SCREENPLAY BY
ARTHUR ROSS AND HARRY ESSEX
FROM A STORY BY MAURICE ZIMM

CREATURE FROM THE Black LAGOON

starring

RICHARD CARLSON · JULIA ADAMS

with

RICHARD DENNING · ANTONIO MORENO
NESTOR PAIVA · WHIT BISSELL

DIRECTED BY JACK ARNOLD · SCREENPLAY BY HARRY ESSEX AND ARTHUR ROSS · PRODUCED BY WILLIAM ALLAND · A UNIVERSAL-INTERNATIONAL PICTURE

LIFE FROM THE SEA

The restless sea!

Life on earth began there. At first, there were only soft animals without backbones in the waters. But then came fish. And from them came amphibians — animals that could swim and also walk on land. Scientists have found fossils of sea-creatures that lived millions of years ago. Some of those fossils look very strange.

They look like they might have belonged to monsters!

One of the greatest horror movies is about such a monster. It had the shape of a man, but it breathed with gills, like a fish. It lived in a mysterious lake deep in the jungle of Brazil.

Its name was the *Creature from the Black Lagoon.*

The story began as a scientist, Dr. Carl Maya, found a very odd fossil.

"That looks like a hand!" said Dr. Maya's helper, Luis.

"But look at the claws!" said the other helper, a younger man named Manuel. "It must have been a real killer."

Dr. Carl Maya (played by Antonio Moreno, right) examines a fossil with his two assistants.

Dr. Maya dug out the fossil hand. He took photos of it. "This fossil could be very important," he said. "I must get help from other scientists before digging up the rest of it. You two stay here and guard the camp. Make sure that no one disturbs the place where the body of the fossil creature is buried."

Luis and Manuel promised to keep a careful watch. Dr. Maya boarded a boat and went off down the jungle river. He planned to go to the Marine Biology Institute. There he would tell other scientists about what he had found.

Wrapped up carefully, lying on the seat beside

him, was the fossil hand with the terrible claws. Dr.
Maya was sure that it had belonged to a creature that
had vanished from the earth millions of years ago.

Back in camp, Luis and Manuel went about their

*Scientists study the fossil. From left to right are David Redd (Richard Carlson),
Kay Lawrence (Julia Adams), Mark Williams (Richard Denning), and John
Thompson (Whit Bissell).*

work. They did not look at the dark waters of the river, where bubbles were rising!

Slowly, from the black depths, came a hand. It was webbed like a frog's and had terrible claws. But this hand was not a fossil. It belonged to something that was alive.

At the Marine Biology Institute, Dr. Maya showed his fossil to other scientists.

The head of the Institute was Dr. Mark Williams. He became very excited. "We must go at once. This is a very important fossil."

Another scientist, Dr. Thompson, said: "The hand almost seems human. Perhaps this creature could help us better understand how life got from the sea to land."

Young Dr. David Reed and his assistant, Kay Lawrence, were also excited by the strange fossil. David was an expert scuba diver. He hoped that they would be able to find many more fossils. Perhaps there would be some in the rocks on the bottom of the river. He decided to bring his scuba gear along.

Dr. Williams hurried to hire a boat. But it was not easy to find a skipper who would go far up the river and agree to stay there with the expedition. That part of the river was feared by the local people. There were legends about it. Legends of monsters.

Finally, Dr. Williams hired Captain Lucas. The captain owned a beat-up old boat called "Rita." It was slow and not very clean. But Lucas was the only skipper who was brave enough, or crazy enough, to go up the mysterious River of the Black Lagoon.

Meanwhile, back in Dr. Maya's camp, night had fallen.

Luis and Manuel were uneasy. The sounds of the jungle were loud one minute, and then suddenly, everything was quiet. The two men looked at each other in fear. Was something outside the tent?

They remembered the old legends. Surely the stories were merely tales to frighten children. But there had been the terrible fossil hand! The hand of a monster that had lived in the water millions of years ago. Dr. Maya had said that such creatures no longer lived on earth. But how could he be certain of that?

Then there was a sound!

It was a growl, like that of the great jungle cat, the jaguar. But, no! It was more like the bellow of a bull alligator. And there were splashing noises.

Something was coming out of the water. Not a jaguar, and not an alligator. Something that walked like a man. It was coming to the tent. Coming to get them.

Luis gave a shout of terror. There at the tent door was an awful face! It had no nose and its mouth was wide, like a frog's. The eyes were fierce and inhuman. Gills sprouted from the creature's head. It reached out toward the two men with great, clawed hands.

One of the men scooped up a kerosene lamp. He threw it at the creature. Burning oil splashed on its scaly body and the thing screeched in pain. It had only been curious before, but now it was full of fury! The men had hurt it, and it would hurt them in return.

As flames from the burning oil lit the dark clearing, Luis and Manuel fought for their lives. They were young and strong.

But the creature was stronger.

The creature comes out of the waters of the Black Lagoon.

14

Dr. Williams and David put on their scuba gear and begin their search for the creature.

The next morning, a boat came chugging up the river. On board were Dr. Maya, Dr. Williams, Dr. Thompson, David and Kay. The skipper, Captain Lucas, steered the boat around a sandbar. Several alligators slid into the water.

Kay moved closer to David. "How big they are. Look at those teeth!"

The boat came to the landing of Dr. Maya's camp. There the expedition found a terrible sight. The tent was burned, and in it were the bodies of Luis and Manuel. But the two men had not died in the fire. They had been clawed to death by some terrible creature.

"Perhaps it was a jaguar," said old Captain Lucas.

His two deckhands, Zee and Chico, looked at each other. Perhaps . . . but there were other horrors that lurked along the River of the Black Lagoon! It was a good thing that the "Rita" had plenty of guns aboard.

Dr. Williams was determined to hunt for the fossil creature in spite of the tragedy. He and David used scuba gear to search the river bottom. Thompson and Kay dug on the shore. They searched for eight days and found no more fossil remains. But Dr. Williams did not want to give up.

"Perhaps Dr. Maya's fossil hand was washed here from upstream," he said. "We must sail further up the river and look there."

Captain Lucas grinned. "At the head of this river is the Black Lagoon. It is said to be a paradise. But no one has ever come back from there alive to prove it!"

Williams sneered at the old boatman. Legends! He told Lucas to sail up the river to the Black Lagoon.

The old boat made its way through a narrow passage. Vine-hung trees grew in the water. Some of the roots scraped the sides of "Rita" as she slowly sailed through. There was barely enough room for the boat to make it.

But at last the narrow channel ended. The scientists looked out over the still waters of the Black Lagoon.

And far back in the swampy shallows, unknown to them, something was watching.

Dr. Williams and David dove with their scuba gear. They searched for rocks on the floor of the lagoon that would tell them how old it was. A net hung over the side of the boat for them to put their specimens in.

They did not know it, but as they swam, the man-shaped water creature followed them.

And later, when Kay went for a peaceful swim in the dark water, the creature followed her, too! The creature was the only one of its kind. It was lonely. Perhaps it thought that Kay was some kind of a female gill-creature. At any rate, it made up its mind to steal her away.

Dr. Williams and David did not know that the creature was following them in the murky waters.

On the boat, Captain Lucas called out to Kay. "Miss Lawrence! Come back! You are too far away!"

He started the boat to come after her and she turned to swim back. Just as she reached the boat, the monster caught up with her.

Kay clambered up the ladder. The gill man, still in the water, began to rock the boat. The scientists who had been in the cabin rushed onto the deck.

"Look! Something is in the net!" cried one.

Captain Lucas started up the motor to haul up the net. Something pulled at the strong meshes, struggling to get away.

While Kay Lawrence is swimming, the gill man almost catches up with her.

The crew finds a large hole and the creature's claw in the net – proof that the creature is alive in the lagoon.

When the net came out of the water, it had a great hole in it. It was empty, except for a single huge claw caught in the mesh.

Dr. Williams ran for his spear gun. "Alive! The fossil creature must be alive here in the Black Lagoon! If we can kill it and take it out of here, we'll become famous!"

David was unhappy with his boss. "We're supposed to be scientists," he said. "We should study the creature alive, not dead."

But Dr. Williams would not listen. As head of the expedition, he could decide what the rest of them must do. He and David put on their scuba gear. Williams took his spear gun and David took an underwater camera. Together they dived down in search of the creature.

The waters of the lagoon were dark. There were many rocks and weeds, and even caverns. The two men searched for the gill man.

And suddenly, they found what they were looking for. The monster appeared! Then it turned to flee with the scientists in pursuit. Williams lifted his spear gun and fired. The sharp harpoon struck the creature and it tumbled in the water. But a moment later it recovered and darted into a deep crevice in the rock.

"Why did you shoot?" David exclaimed, when he and Dr. Williams came to the surface. "It looked human!"

But all Williams could think about was killing the creature and taking its body back to civilization. Of course, it was not human. It was an animal. And somehow or other, he was going to find it and kill it.

Dr. Williams injures the creature with his spear gun.

The creature sneaks aboard the boat while everyone is asleep.

That night, an awful thing happened. The deckhand named Chico was dragged overboard and drowned — by something.

"The demon has killed my brother!" shouted the other boatman, Zee. "You must do something!"

When it was light, Captain Lucas made plans of his own. "I have a chemical," he told David. "It is called rotenone. We use it to stun fish so that we can catch them easily. If we put rotenone into the Black Lagoon, perhaps the demon will suffocate."

The scientists eagerly waited while Lucas put the chemical into the water. Hundreds of stunned fish floated to the surface.

But no gill man.

Night fell. The people on the boat remained alert in case the creature should appear. Suddenly they heard a noise. A spotlight on the "Rita" shone into the jungle. There was the creature, standing in the shallows! David and Dr. Williams rushed after it.

The creature fled and tried to hide in a cave. But the scientists found it and wounded it with spear guns. Crazy with pain, the creature came to the shore where Kay was standing. It grabbed her. Zee ran to help Kay, but the creature leaped on him and killed him.

The creature attacks Kay, but she is saved by a brave deckhand.

The other men rushed up with a net and cast it over the monster. At last, the terrible demon of the Black Lagoon was captured.

Imprisoned in a strong bamboo cage was a legend come to life: a thing that seemed to be part man and part fish. Its cage had to be kept hanging in the water, because the creature breathed with gills like a fish.

The men look at the creature they have captured in their net.

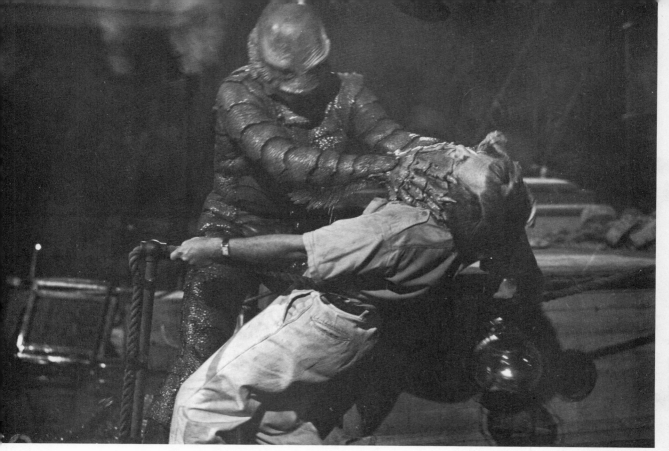

The gill man attacks Dr. Thompson.

Dr. Williams thought that the monster would be safe in the cage. But he was wrong. The gill man broke free. It attacked Dr. Thompson and injured him seriously, then escaped into the water of the lagoon.

"Enough is enough," exclaimed David. "We must get out of here. Four men are already dead and poor Thompson is badly hurt."

"No!" said Dr. Williams. "We can't leave until we get that creature — dead or alive!"

But Captain Lucas had the last word. Drawing a knife, he gently held it to Dr. Williams' neck. "On water, the captain makes the decisions," he said. "And I say that we're going home."

They pulled up "Rita's" anchor and started the engine. The old boat chugged to the channel leading out of the Black Lagoon. And there it had to stop. The channel was blocked by a sunken snag.

It was the work of the monster.

The creature, mad with fury, tried to climb into the boat. The people on board seized guns and fired at the monster, driving it away. Then they tried to drag the obstacle away from the boat, using the winch.

But every time they put a cable around the sunken snag, the monster would unfasten it. David and Dr. Williams went into the water to drive it away and the gill man attacked them.

In a furious underwater struggle, Dr. Williams was killed and David had to retreat back into the boat. The exit of the lagoon was still blocked.

"There is some rotenone left," said Captain Lucas. "We could use it to keep the demon away while we shift the logs."

As they mixed up the last of the chemical inside the boat's cabin, a scaly arm came through a porthole! It grabbed at poor Dr. Thompson, who lay bandaged on a bunk. Kay screamed: "It's come back!"

Kay warns everyone that the creature is attacking Dr. Thompson.

The creature climbs back aboard while everyone looks the other way.

David leaped up and slashed at the arm with a long knife. The creature dropped back into the water. "This rotenone had better work," he said.

Armed with the chemical, David descended into the lagoon and once more fastened the cable to the snag. The creature came swimming at him — but a squirt of the rotenone drove the gill man off.

David came to the surface. "Now start the winch!" he cried.

The Captain began to reel in the cable, but the sunken tree was too heavy. "We will back up the boat," he decided. This time, the underwater obstacle moved. In a few moments the channel was open. "Now we can get out of here," David said.

But he was speaking too soon. While those on board the "Rita" had watched the clearing of the channel, the creature managed to climb into the boat again.

It grabbed Kay, and swam away.

Dr. Maya and the Captain fire at the creature inside its cave.

The gill man brought Kay to its cave on the shore. David followed and found Kay there, unharmed. As David took Kay into his arms to comfort her, he heard a growl. The creature had returned to its victim.

Bellowing with rage, it attacked David. The scientist and the gill man fell to the cave floor. The creature's hands, with their terrible claws, reached for David's throat.

Suddenly shots rang out. The creature staggered, then began to run. Lucas and Dr. Maya, who had followed David, chased the monster back toward the lagoon, firing at the scaly form.

David and Kay followed. The young scientist was grateful to Maya and Lucas for rescuing them, but his mind was still in a turmoil. If only there were some way to avoid killing the creature! It had attacked them only when it felt threatened by human beings.

"Wait!" cried David. Lucas and Dr. Maya had their rifles raised, ready to fire again. They were ready to deliver the killing shots, but they paused at David's shout.

The creature rushed toward the lagoon and fell in with a great splash. The dark waters closed over its body. It sank slowly . . . slowly . . . down into its home in the Black Lagoon.

The survivors watch the moratally wounded creature sink into the Black Lagoon.

The captured creature floats in the tank as though it is dead.

REVENGE OF THE CREATURE

The movie *Creature from the Black Lagoon* was a great hit. One year after it was issued in 1954, Universal Pictures produced a similar film, *Revenge of the Creature.*

Another group of scientists came to the Black

Lagoon. And this time, they managed to capture the gill man alive!

Stunned by its ordeal, the creature was taken to a seaquarium in Florida and put into a tank. People gaped as scientists moved the scaly monster through the water, trying to revive it. Perhaps the creature was dead! But its flippered limbs twitched. Its gills fluttered.

It began to breathe, to move, to climb out of the tank!

Screaming people scattered in all directions. Seaquarium guards struck at the raging creature with boathooks. It fell back into its tank. And from then on, it was chained when it was shown to the excited public.

The scientist who had captured the gill man brought his girlfriend to see it. The poor monster, perhaps longing for a mate once again, decided that she was its heart's desire.

The lonely creature kidnaps the scientist's girlfriend.

The creature tips over a car on the beach.

Later, the creature broke free of its chains and escaped into the Florida night. It prowled the waterfront, looking for its unsuspecting human love.

Tracking the scientist and the woman to a restaurant, the creature managed to carry off its sweetheart. However, the monster could not keep its victim because it had to return to the water in order to stay alive.

Left on shore, the woman escaped. And a gun-toting crowd of rescuers chased the lovelorn creature off in a hail of bullets.

Once again, an apparently dying gill man sank into the black depths. But again, it was destined to return.

THE CREATURE WALKS AMONG US

The third and last of the movies featuring the gill man appeared in 1956.

In this film, scientists discover that the fishy critter had not died after all. It was alive and well, and living in the Florida swamps. Naturally, they had to track it down. And as always, they underestimated its power.

Enraged by attempts to capture it, the creature tries to upset the scientists' boat. As in the original

The gill man tries to escape from the scientists.

movie, a kerosene lamp is thrown. The gill man is again engulfed in flames. This time the burns are severe enough to render the gill man harmless. It is taken to a laboratory for treatment.

X-rays show that the creature is far more human than the scientists had suspected. Inside its chest are hidden lungs. The scientists connect these up and remove the creature's gills — changing it from a water-breather to an air-breather.

The scientists bandage the creature's burns.

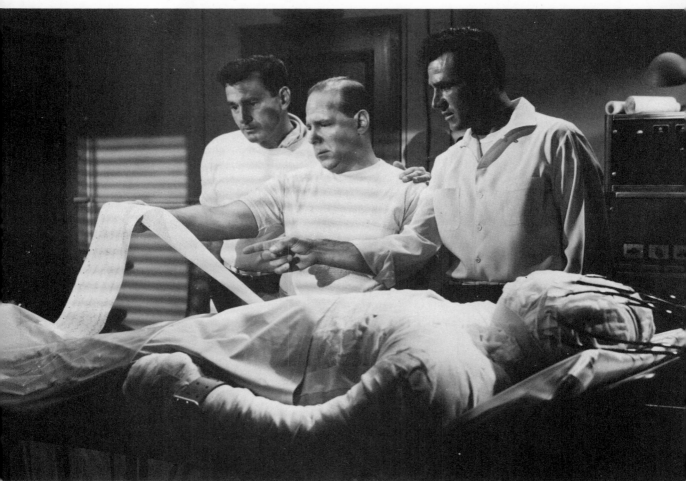

The nearly human creature escapes to the sea and drowns.

The scaly body is also changed into semi-human shape. When the monster recovers from its burns, it becomes mild-mannered. Dressed in an ill-fitting suit of clothes, it mopes around in a laboratory pen and stares longingly at the sea. And then a beautiful woman comes on the scene.

It is a case of monster meets girl, monster loves girl. The hopeless romance reaches a high point when villains threaten the life of the woman. The creature bursts through an electrified fence and destroys the evil-doers.

Seeing that its loved one is safe, the creature makes a sad exit. It walks into the dawn-lit sea, where it is certain to drown now that its gills have been re-placed with lungs.

THE MAKING OF THE CREATURE

The original *Creature from the Black Lagoon* was a 3-D movie. This film process was popular during the 1950's. The viewer wore a pair of cardboard eyeglasses with one red and one green lens. The picture on the screen was projected in a double image of green and red. When viewed through the special glasses, the movie seemed to "come alive."

Monsters seemed to leap right off the screen at the audience! The scene was not flat, but realistic — with three dimensions. The actors seemed to be living, rounded persons.

A 3-D movie makes you feel as though you are a part of the story.

Julia Adams and Richard Carlson, co-stars of CREATURE FROM THE BLACK LAGOON.

It is still possible to see these old 3-D movies in modern theaters. And they are still a lot of fun! The sequel, *Revenge of the Creature,* was also made in 3-D. But the third movie in the series went back to the old flat-screen process when the 3-D fad faded away.

If you see the *Creature from the Black Lagoon* as a television movie, you will see it in a flat-screen version. It is still a horror classic, mainly because of the splendid job of makeup and costume used in portraying the monster.

One of the greatest makeup experts of all time, Bud Westmore, was in charge of the "Creature Project." He knew that he would not be able to use the ordinary kinds of paint and glued-on pieces to create the gilled creature. The monster would have to be sturdy enough to swim, and fight. The stunt man who played the role would have to wear a very special "monster suit" — one that was different from any makeup or costume ever made before.

The stunt man practices with Julia Adams during rehearsal.

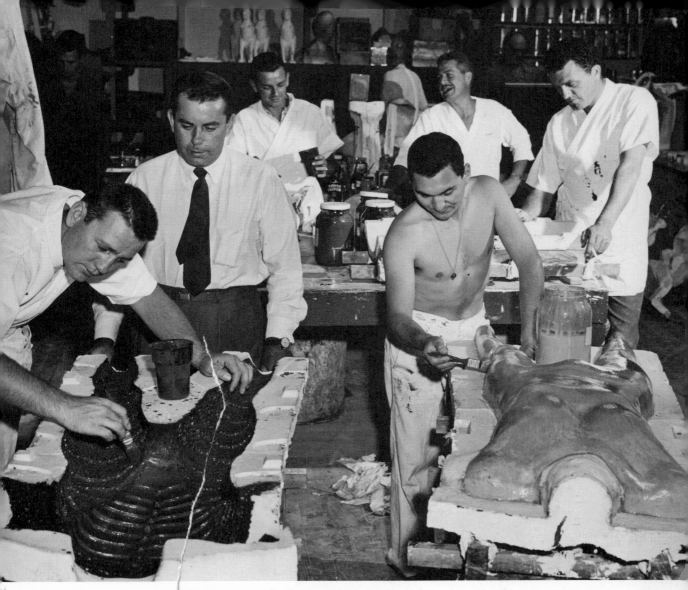

It took many people to make the gill man costume.

Westmore's crew began by making a clay statue of the creature, life sized. It had the head and gills of a fish, froglike hands and feet, and a scaled body rather like that of an alligator. From this statue molds were made for the head, torso, and limbs of the rubber creature costume.

Pieces taken from their molds after baking were colored. Such things as scales and claws were cemented in place. Then the rubber pieces were carefully fitted to the body of the stunt man who would portray the creature in the film. The "monster suit" fit as closely as a second skin. Wearing them, the stunt man hardly looked like a human being at all!

Millicent Patrick designed the gill man's mask.

The creature's "feet" also had to be specially designed.

In the first Black Lagoon movie, Ben Chapman was the creature during the scenes shot on land. In the underwater scenes, Ricou Browning took over. Browning was an expert swimmer who could hold his breath for five minutes. This was very important — because a real gill-breather would never give off bubbles! (When the stunt man needed air, he would take a swig from an air-hose bubbling away out of camera range.)

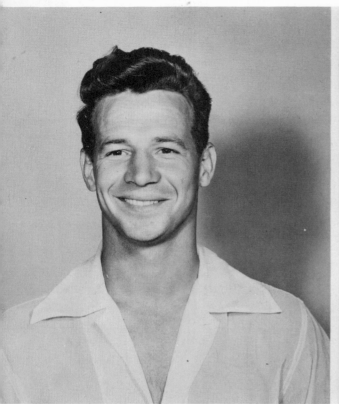

On the left is Ricou Browning, an expert underwater swimmer. On the right Mr. Browning wears the gill man costume.

Browning alone played the gill man in *Revenge of the Creature*. He developed a special "monstrous" style of swimming for the role that was very impressive.

As he glided through the water, claws outstretched, it was easy to believe that he really belonged to the world of the deep. He was graceful — almost attractive — as long as he stayed in the water, not bothered by people.

It was only when the creature was taken from his Black Lagoon and forced to live on land that he became a monster.

Camera crews also had to work underwater to film the creature.